Music Lessons for Children
with Special Needs

of related interest

**Movement Activities for Children
    with Learning Difficulties**
Bren Pointer
ISBN 1 85302 167 9

Odyssey Now
Nicola Grove and Keith Park
ISBN 1 85302 315 9

Children with Special Needs
Assessment, Law and Practice –
Caught in the Acts, 3rd Edition
John Friel
ISBN 1 85302 280 2

**Making Music with the Young Child
    with Special Needs**
A Guide for Parents
Elaine Streeter
ISBN 1 85302 187 3

Music Lessons for Children with Special Needs

T. M. Perry

Jessica Kingsley Publishers
London and Bristol, Pennsylvania

First published in the United Kingdom in 1995 by
Jessica Kingsley Publishers Ltd
116 Pentonville Road
London N1 9JB, England
and
1900 Frost Road, Suite 101
Bristol, PA 19007, U S A

Copyright © 1995 T.M. Perry

Library of Congress Cataloging in Publication Data
A CIP catalogue record for this book is available from the Library of Congress

British Library Cataloguing in Publication Data
A CIP catalogue record for this book is available from the British Library

ISBN 1-85302-295-0

Printed and Bound in Great Britain by
Biddles Ltd, Guildford and King's Lynn

Contents

With profound thanks
to the staff and pupils
of the Sanderling Unit,
Rock Ferry High School,
Rock Ferry, Birkenhead,
Merseyside

Introduction

This book was conceived as an aid to the organisation of my teaching when faced with mixed groups of children who displayed a wide range of learning difficulties. Although they were aged from 11 to 16 years, my pupils often performed at levels which would be regarded as average for children two or three years younger, and I came reluctantly to accept that their achievements were as much a measure of my failings as of any that might be attributed to them.

Whatever our shortcomings, my pupils seemed at most times to be enjoying their musical experiences, and if the capacity for the enjoyment of music were made a part of a child's profile of attainment, then I would expect that they would achieve a comparable standing, at the very least, with their peers in mainstream schools.

I write then, not as an expert, but as an experienced teacher with ideas which may be of value and interest to others. Furthermore, I write, think, and teach from the point of view that the teacher is the most important resource in the classroom, and that without an effective channel of communication between teacher and pupils, no positive learning can take place. It is the primary task of the teacher to create and maintain communication with his or her class, and to demonstrate at all times that teaching and learning are mutually dependent aspects of development: theirs – and yours.

The lessons visit all the Programmes of Study of the National Curriculum, but, as in my own scheme of work, the emphasis is different. I aim to adjust my lessons and my teaching to suit particular groups of pupils and individual needs. My overall scheme retains the division between Attainment Targets 1 and 2, but places the eight strands into four areas of activity. For children with learning difficulties it is essential that the aims of the music teacher are wide-ranging and eclectic. You may want to focus on hand–eye co-ordination with a particular child, or on aural practice with another; or to help a child get used to working, and eventually performing, with a group. In such cases music is the medium, but the teacher's objectives are projected far beyond the musical activity.

My objectives, then, are tailored to suit each of my pupils, and my overall aim is to contribute to the growth and effective development of each of them. I am certainly not going to make musicians of my pupils in the 35 minutes a week that is allotted to them, but I hope to enrich them in some way, and to reinforce and support work that they are doing in other subject areas. You must decide what your pupils need in your lessons, and perhaps begin by projecting the sort of lessons you would like to deliver if there were no restrictions on time, resources, and the sizes of your teaching groups. From there, compromise where you must; but remember that although it is your pupils' individual development that is paramount, yours cannot be compromised.

It will be of no value to your pupils to sacrifice your own stability to a misplaced ideal. Children want to be taught by someone who is strict, but fair and able to listen; serious, but ready to laugh at appropriate moments; and perhaps most of all, by someone who is energetic, caring, and full of ideas.

Teachers in special education have to cope with constant re-evaluation of the names given to categories of children with special needs. The latest applied by the local authority to the pupils that I teach is 'complex learning difficulties', which is more accurate, and more honest, than some of the names which preceded it. The problem for the teacher is that the new category can include children with special needs for whom provision was previously made in a wide variety of educational institutions, and teaching becomes a presentation of sometimes quite different strategies. You also may be faced with a group containing a child with emotional and behavioural problems; another with a physical disability; another who has problems with language, or with spatial relationships, or with co-ordination; another who is withdrawn, and unable to relate to other children; and another who is pleasant, affable, and full of smiles, but who never seems to understand the lesson.

All of these children will have emotional problems, and may present in unique ways. Your task is to steer a course as close to your ideals as possible, without placing your sanity at risk, in what often may appear as a storm of conflicting emotions.

Remember that you are the principal resource in the classroom, and that your presentation and classroom management are crucial to the success of your lessons. Neither the subject, nor instruments, nor text books, recordings or videos should be allowed to detract from your status and authority as teacher. This is not to say that you should be authoritarian, but that you should be seen to manage the sessions so that things happen according to your design; although you will, of course, be receptive at all times to the moods, needs, and desires of the class:

- It is essential that you begin each lesson with a clear idea of what you are going to do, and what you hope the children will achieve: but you must always have an alternative plan in mind, even if it consists only of improvising with the percussion instruments, or singing songs from memory.

- Before you meet the group, you should if possible arrange the furniture to suit your plan, taking into consideration the social structure of the group: which children cannot sit together; where eye contact between children is to be discouraged, and so on. When you meet your pupils, you tell them where you want them to sit, and in subsequent lessons, by trial and error, you should arrive at a satisfactory seating plan and stick to it.

- What you are going to do, and the responses that you expect from your pupils, should be made clear by every practical means. You will speak to the class using gestures, and body language; you may support your oral presentation by writing, or drawing on the blackboard; you may demonstrate on an instrument; you may offer words, music, or pictures on paper; or on a recording; but it is essential that your communication is multi-dimensional, and multi-sensory.

You will know that encouragement is a vital feature of the learning and teaching process, but try to be realistic about it. If a child is floundering, it is of little value to offer praise, and to urge him or her on to greater effort. You must be ready at a moment's notice to break down a task into more manageable units, and you will become skilled at doing so without the child feeling that he or she has failed. Try the original task yourself, for instance, and stumble, or appear to struggle as if you have suddenly realised how difficult it is. You may not even need to pretend! Then break it down, and offer the less onerous task; perhaps with a joke, and an apology.

Few activities will hold your pupils' attention for more than ten minutes, although there will always be someone who wants to carry on. Remember that, whatever you decide in such circumstances, you will soon enough be confronted with the child who says: 'You let him do it last time, now you won't let me!' There will be times when you must deny individuals the opportunity to carry on – perhaps even when they have success within their grasp – in order to maintain group unity, and to sustain your authority; and other times when it may be convenient, for similar reasons, to allow one or two children extra time at a popular activity. You are the arbiter: you must make your decision, explain it, and stick by it, preferably without a confrontation with others in the group. The most effective strategy is to make sure that the next activity promises to be more fun than the last.

Egocentric attitudes and irrational comments are a function of the teacher–class equilibrium. Remember how it felt the last time you were undergoing in-service training, and a trainer spoke patronisingly to the group? Try to stay calm if a child sets out to provoke you with unfair comment, and, if the child persists, make arrangements to speak privately to him or her as soon as possible: certainly no later than the end of the lesson.

There should be a school or unit policy for such situations, but unless the child has a record of persistent naughtiness, this is not the time for admonishment. You should place yourself so that you can maintain eye contact; ask for an explanation of the child's behaviour; and leave lots of space after the child's answer. Naughty children are most often unhappy or insecure at home, and, although it may be helpful for you to know something of their problems, you should not ask too many questions, or try to pry too deeply into their lives beyond school. If a child is able to talk freely without feeling disloyal to his or her parents, then you are obliged to respond sympathetically on those terms. Ultimately, however, you can offer care and comfort only within the school system, and you should try, as gently as possible, to persuade the aggrieved personality before you that your efforts are devoted to the well-being of all the children in the class, and that it is unfair that one individual should disrupt the education of others on a regular basis.

When you make mistakes, try to learn without carrying an extra parcel of negative emotion. Children quickly forget things that went wrong, when offered enjoyable experiences at which they can succeed, and they do not normally bear grudges if you are able to show with an apology, and your subsequent behaviour, that you too have learnt from a mistake.

Communication throughout lessons should be multi-sensory. You must be ready to put fingers into the correct places on keyboards, or to move them in sequence to demonstrate a pattern; but you should never touch a child who either pulls away or shows an unnatural response to being touched. You may need to hold a child's hands, wrists, or arms from behind to show how it feels to play a drum in time, or to walk an awkward child through a dance or marching routine – but gently does it. You have no right to impose your will, only to support, guide, and enable a child who is receptive to your teaching.

You should cultivate the skill of representing patterns of sound or movement on the blackboard with graphic images, or, if you do not have the time or skills, search out illustrations from magazines which reinforce the point that you are trying to make. A constant theme in your teaching might be that patterns or sequences exist all around us, as well as in every subject area in school; and that patterns are organic; constantly growing, changing, and taking on new forms.

The teacher's position in the classroom is a vital part of the communication process, and closely allied to the grouping and placing of the pupils. There is a lot to be said in traditional pedagogy for the rows of desks or tables and chairs facing the teacher, but, for most practical music lessons with a small group of children with special needs, a more informal arrangement is more suitable. I find it safest, for lessons with electronic keyboards, to arrange the tables round three sides of a rectangle, with all leads and connections in the centre, away from stumbling feet, and helping hands. This works well for other lessons as well, since I am left with a useful space at the rear of the room where I can set up percussion instruments, and organise activities involving movement. When I want to direct a group activity I may do so from the fourth side of the rectangle, which is provided by my desk, standing a few feet away from the blackboard. I spend most of my keyboard lessons, however, moving from pupils to pupil round the rectangle, and it is during individual interaction that I regard my most valuable work as taking place.

To make the most of your presence in the classroom you must keep moving, not only with the aim of helping and encouraging, but also to forestall frustration and jealousy, and to create the illusion that you are omnipresent:

- You will find that more able children may need little direct assistance, but often want you to listen to their work, and although this can be a pleasant and rewarding activity for both parties, you should make sure that all your pupils receive an equal share of your time and attention.

- In particular, do not forget those quiet children who never speak unless in answer to a direct question. Not only are they entitled to your attention as much as any more extrovert child, but such children can be powerful allies in your strategies for classroom management. Much depends on their social standing within the group, but a good-natured and passive child can often be a calming influence on others who are excitable, or too demanding.

The teacher's language, and the tone and style of delivery, are perhaps the most important aspect of communication with the class, if only because of the childrens' expectations, and the immediacy of the contact. At your first meeting with a group you should begin to define some of the terms you will be using, making sure that you speak simply and clearly with lots of examples to support your definitions. Many children, for instance, think of a song as a complete performance, with accompaniment, on a record. When you give instructions, use gestures, and facial expressions alongside your words, and always introduce a new activity with a demonstration.

Although it is important to agree on the meanings of key words in music – the names of instruments, for instance, and such terms as melody, harmony, rhythm and pulse – there will be scope for expressive language when you begin to talk about the tone and timbre of instruments, the sounds that groups of them produce, and the effects they may create. You must make a point of encouraging your pupils to find words to describe musical experiences. Unless they are plainly illogical, or deliberately perverse, you should display their suggestions, and try to use them in subsequent discussions. You might, for instance, ask a class to match colours with different sounds, and to justify their selections to the group; and you should let your pupils hear some examples of expressive language in your descriptions of the recorded music they are about to hear. Most opportunities will occur, however, in your practical class routines. Drums thud, for instance, and a good drummer can drive a group along. Glockenspiels tinkle, and sound like fairy bells; brass instruments may snort and roar; tambourines can rattle and tremble; and a tightly held triangle just goes dink.

It will often be necessary for you to demonstrate a musical sound or effect. You should practise doing so with humility, unless of course you are demonstrating the sort of presentation that sells records. In general, your pupils will expect you to be quietly competent on all the classroom instruments, and your aim should be to show how natural and easy it is to make real music, without leaving them thinking that they can never aspire to such brilliance. Perform, but do not show off!

Not only is each classroom a unique world, but you will find that each of your classes is different even when the names on your register are the same. This is not just because of the varied content of your lessons, but because of the variable currents of emotion from your pupils, and the linked tidal system of your emotional state and theirs. The key to successful classroom management, and the successful teaching of children with special needs, is your relationships with your pupils:

- You will find that although teachers are often used by children as surrogate parents, or as referred adults to whom they can transfer transient but strong emotions, your most effective role is as teacher.

- You must accept what they give, neither welcome nor reject emotion, and seek at all times to open a channel of expectancy between you and the children.

- They must know that your efforts are devoted to their well-being and development, and that you believe their best interests to be served by a positive attitude to lessons in school, even when lessons fall below expectations for one reason or another, and you know that you have not been at your best.

- You must be self-critical; keep a log or a diary of your lessons with comments; and try not to use a difficult child, or class, as an excuse for your failures.

The scheme of the teaching suggested in this book may be visualised as a spiral, the basic elements recurring at different levels, or perhaps with different emphasis each time. The first few lessons are designed to be used with new and inexperienced groups, but beyond that there is no particular significance in the order. I have suggested ideas, and occasionally directions, for extending the activities, but the lessons are there to be modified, and used according to the needs of the teacher and the children. It is inevitable that for some children the spiral will take on a narrow, flat, or lopsided shape, but teachers who work through all the lessons will at least know that they have presented a comprehensive view of the subject area.

CHAPTER 1

A Music Scheme of Work for Pupils with Special Needs

The National Curriculum Attainment Targets (abbreviated to AT in the text) are: 1. Performing and Composing; and 2. Listening and Appraising. There are Programmes of Study relating to the Attainment Targets in each of Key Stages 1, 2 and 3, but at Key Stage 4 public examinations are the intended means by which attainment may be assessed.

In the Scheme of Work which follows I have expressed the requirements of the National Curriculum Programmes of Study in terms of four areas of activity as follows:

Attainment Target 1

1. Melody; singing and playing

2. Rhythm

3. Communicating

Attainment Target 2

4. Listening and responding

AT1. MELODY; SINGING AND PLAYING

At the keyboard: tunes using five notes with appropriate fingering; the five note scale, and tunes using scale or arpeggio passages. Patterns in melody and phrase. Dynamics, timbre and pace. Relating a melody to words. Playing solo in front of a group, and playing a part in a group performance. Improvising a melody in response to a stimulus. Playing a tune by ear, as well as from note names and traditional notation. Fitting melodies to a pulse or rhythmic accompaniment.

Singing in a group; singing a solo part or line, and taking part in simple antiphonal and canonic arrangements. Recognising, remembering, and reproducing simple tunes and songs.

AT1. RHYTHM

Responding to a rhythmic stimulus: moving in time; clapping hands or stamping feet to copy or echo a rhythm pattern. Beating time on percussion instruments, using a variety of beaters, and right, or left, or both hands. Marching in response to a strong pulse, and simple dance movements. Using the metronome; fitting rhythm patterns over a pulse. Using the heartbeat as a stimulus.

Improvising percussion patterns to fit a mood, or a melody. Choosing the sounds, and mixing texture, timbre, and pitch. Making music with pitched and unpitched percussion.

AT1. COMMUNICATING

Composing and performing to a group using any combination of sound and rhythm. Using microphone or video recorder to record work. Using note names, traditional notation or graphic notation to record work.

Setting words to music; finding or making music to fit words. Making pictures on video, or using graphic media to accompany music; making or selecting music to accompany pictures.

Conducting an ensemble: improvising music in response to a stimulus; selecting and controlling the texture, density, and volume of sound; organising a group performance.

AT2. LISTENING AND RESPONDING

Listening to local sounds: to familiar noises, and to music on television, radio, and records. Famous, familiar, and popular music selected according to a theme or topic. Responding to a musical stimulus orally, or graphically, or through movement, or composition.

Learning to recognise patterns, and structures in recorded music; and being aware of AB; AABA; and ABC forms – particularly in popular song.

Learning the sounds and names of a wide range of musical instruments, and the principles of sound production.

Listening to simple harmonic structures, and discriminating between chords I; IV; and V.

The Lessons Related to the Scheme of Work

AT 1. Singing and Playing	AT 1. Rhythm	AT 1. Communicating	AT 2. Listening and Responding
1.			
2.			
	3.		
	4.		
5.	5.		
	6.		
7.			
	8.		
		9.	
	10.		
11.			
		12.	12.
		13.	
14.			
		15.	15.
16.	16.	16.	16.
			17.
		18.	18.
		19.	19.
			20.

THE LESSONS – A SUMMARY

Lesson 1. Getting to know a group; singing songs that they know from memory; singing a round, and a song with actions.

Lesson 2. First exercises on keyboards or pitched percussion; playing a simple tune from note names.

Lesson 3. Finding a pulse and reproducing it on percussion; increasing and decreasing tempo; managing beaters.

Lesson 4. Foot tapping in time; counting beats, and marching on the spot; then round the room. Playing a drum in time and marching.

Lesson 5. The heartbeat played as an ostinato on xylophones using the pentatonic scale.

Lesson 6. Rhythmic patterns clapped, and then performed on percussion; echoing patterns; questions and answers with the instruments.

Lesson 7. Five finger exercises at the keyboards; practising and performing a five note tune.

Lesson 8. Playing small percussion instruments and passing them around the group following the teacher's cues from the piano or keyboard.

Lesson 9. First steps in conducting; conducting an improvised piece of percussion music.

Lesson 10. Counting and playing percussion instruments on particular beats; leading to an eight-part ensemble.

Lesson 11. Fingering a scale at the keyboard; discerning the pitch of a motif, and the direction of the notes; performing a simple tune together.

Lesson 12. Listening to music: a descriptive or narrative piece of orchestral music; responding with artwork; finding words to talk about the music.

Lesson 13. First steps in composition; putting three notes into a pleasing rhythmic order, or improvising a pattern; altering notes of a familiar tune.

Lesson 14. Singing together; reading words, chanting them in time; finding soloists and a chorus.

Lesson 15. Group activities; rhythm exercises and games.

Lesson 16. Group performances of vocal or instrumental pieces using soloists and accompanists; competing groups or choruses; practising and recording a performance.

Lesson 17. Shape, pattern and form; parallels with artwork; a graphic response to a piece of recorded music, responding to its form.

Lesson 18. Musical notation; traditional forms, and graphic notation; devising shapes and sound to represent them – and vice versa.

Lesson 19. Musical form: putting together elements of sound to make a composition using recorded or improvised samples.

Lesson 20. The expressive and emotive potential of sound; examples from the environment; personal associations and meanings.

CHAPTER 2

The Lessons

Lesson 1
Introducing Melody
Through Singing

It is characteristic of some children with special needs that they have particular difficulty in reproducing models of patterns that they have seen or heard. Playing even a simple melody like *Twinkle Twinkle* poses at least a two-dimensional problem; setting aside for the moment problems of tempo, timbre, and memory, the pupil has to find the correct notes, and play them in at least a close approximation of the correct rhythm before the tune is recognisable. Furthermore the task is sometimes made more difficult because the child does not know the tune well, and this may be difficult to ascertain because often children will say that they know something to please a teacher, or simply to be left alone. It is safest for the teacher to teach even the simplest of tunes, before asking children to match letter names to patterns of pitch and rhythm.

- With a new class at your first meeting, sing to them, and find out what songs they may know. Sing to encourage a response, and to suggest an agenda for the lesson – but not to show off your voice, or to demonstrate your performing skills.

- Sing nursery rhymes and ask them for help with the words. With older children suggest that they imagine singing to a younger brother or sister. This lesson should be without piano accompaniment throughout.

- Perform a nursery rhyme as a group. Introduce a round, and explain the form. Do they know *London's Burning*? If not, teach the song, write the words on a board to remind them, and perform it in two groups – perhaps you and the class.

- Introduce a song with movement, or actions *I Am The Music Man*, or *Underneath The Spreading Chestnut Tree*, for instance. The extroverts in the group will probably become more prominent now, and they – or perhaps only he, or she – should be encouraged in a matter-of-fact way without implying that they are superior to the rest of the class.

- Sit among the children and enjoy the performance, join in the choruses and the actions, and try to make mental note of pupils who seem to have problems in remembering what comes next, or in co-ordinating their movements.

Keep a journal, or a log of all lessons. Write down briefly what you did, how successful it was, and how it may be improved next time. And make notes about the pupils, in your own shorthand or code, so that each activity adds to your bank or information about specific problems and needs.

Lesson 2
Melody at the Keyboard (1)

When a tune can be sung – perhaps only to La – then the pupil may attempt to reproduce it on a keyboard or tuned percussion. This next step is a major hurdle for many children. Without speculating as to which areas of the brain are involved, it is certain that finding letter names written on keys, and pressing the keys with a finger, are activities profoundly different from what follows. The pupils must perceive the resulting pattern of pitch and compare it with an internal model, then simultaneously draw on a separate rhythmic model, before they are able to generate the appropriate commands to the fingers that are doing the pressing.

To those of us for whom simple tunes appear as natural and as obvious as leaves, it is sometimes hard to appreciate the problems faced by children who seem to find the essentially interlocking parts of a tune as separate and even optional. Opportunities for confusion occur at every stage of the learning process, and it is important that the teacher at least is aware of the potential obstacles, and is able to recognise the different demands made on the pupil at each stage of a musical task.

Make sure that each child has a keyboard or melody instrument with the note names clearly marked.

Choose a note and ask them to play it three, four, or five times. Welcome the noise! Ask one or two children each time to play together, either after an introductory count, or in response to your conducting. Demonstrate by singing; exaggerate the beat, with a clearly defined upbeat in tempo. Repeat the activity still using repeated notes of the same pitch, but with a distinction between long and short, and perhaps between very long and very short. Notice children who lose count easily; who have problems distinguishing between long and short; or whose performance appears to be affected by emotional cross-currents within the group.

Choose a group of adjacent notes; sing them to the class after an introductory count, and ask them to pattern the sound on their instruments. Watch finger movements carefully and suggest early on that consecutive notes be played with adjacent fingers if possible.

Children are often hampered in their appreciation of the shape of a tune if they try to play it using one index finger alone, whereas if the tonic note is always played with the thumb, this will encourage a tactile, as well as audible, sense of tonality.

Count; and conduct a performance. If the children are playing keyboards with alternative voices, suggest that they each choose a different sound, and ask for individual performances. Point out the difference between legato and percussive versions of the melody.

Give the note names of a simple tune such as *Twin-kle Twinkle* preferably on paper or card propped up before them, and on the blackboard as well. Play the tune to them first, then give them a few minutes to practise it. Depending on the mood of the group, hear either a group performance, or individual perform-ances. It is one of the music teacher's most difficult tasks to promote confidence in pupils on the one hand and, on the other, to keep in check the extrovert's desire to show off.

To clarify the task:

1. The child is taught a tune by singing and playing: with or without words; and with strongly accented rhythm, reinforced if possible by movement.

2. The child is shown the *tessitura* of the tune on a keyboard or tuned percussion with clearly marked notes, then given the note names of the tune and asked to reproduce the tune.

3. The notes alone will not pattern the tune. Remind pupils of the rhythm, and of the dimension of tempo. A tune played too fast or too slow, or with exaggerated rubato, will not be recognisable. This is the crucial stage at which a child's confidence may be reinforced or crushed. Help them with fingering; singing, beating the rhythm, or even putting their fingers down on the keys to help establish a kinaesthetic pattern.

4. The reproduction of a complete tune may be beyond some children, perhaps because of an inability to memorise note names and patterns, or because of a limited span of concentration. Try to establish a complete performance of the tune as soon as possible, even if it means dividing it up so that some children only play a few notes.

5. Conduct the tune, mistakes and all, beating time, and singing along with the group. Emphasise the pulse, and sequential patterns, particularly of rhythm, which for many children takes precedence over pitch. Avoid accompanying them on the piano at first as this puts you behind a physical barrier, and across a cultural divide.

Lesson 3
Rhythm from the Pulse

Ask the children to feel their wrists for their pulse, and to communicate the beat to you by vocalising. If no pulse is evident, help them to find it and encourage the vocalisation. Establish the idea of tunes having a basic pulse like a heartbeat, over which a rhythmic pattern may be superimposed.

Do a simple percussion exercise in which each child reproduces his or her pulse on an instrument. Ask a lively child to run on the spot for a minute or so, and then listen to his or her pulse again. Ask the child to demonstrate the effect of a quickening pulse on a drum, followed by the pulse returning to normal. Try this as a group exercise, and conduct the tempo changes, or get the children to take it in turns with the baton.

Most children are able to manage changes in tempo with ease and enjoyment; it is when the teacher asks for half speed or double speed beats to be superimposed over the basic pulse that difficulties most often become obvious. It is as if the teacher has asked them to make a pencil and paper calculation. You must show them how the pulse of a simple tune may be simplified and adapted for two players; with the bass drum, for instance playing two in a four-four bar; and a side drum playing the pulse. Then move on to try another instrument joining in with the off beats, and ask your pupils to try and count fours as they play or listen.

You must take particular care to observe the children's movements as they manipulate the beaters and sticks. Some who have difficulty playing in time may be processing the results of their actions too slowly, or reacting too late even though they are aware of the problem. Some children with perceptual problems may cock their heads to one side as if straining to hear the pulse, while others who seem to have no sense of rhythm at all either stand like coiled springs waiting for a message to arrive, or, at the other extreme, like rag dolls, striking out at the drum at random, and sometimes missing altogether. You must support them with sensitivity and gentle humour: hold their hands with the sticks in them if necessary, and help them to a physical recognition of what it means to play in time. Because playing in front of an audience can be very stressful you must invent clapping games for your group to try together so that shortcomings are not thrown into high relief.

Remember above all, that a child who does not perceive or react to rhythm will not know what you mean by 'playing in time'. You must bring your pupils to a real knowledge of what it means, by visual, aural, and tactile experience. Your task is to play; sing the beats; clap your hands; stamp your feet; move your body in time to the pulse; and encourage your pupils to do the same.

Lesson 4
Rhythmic Movement

All activities in which children are asked to make noises pose problems of class management. All such activities described or suggested here may need to be curtailed, or modified, in deference to the needs of everyone concerned – not least yourself. When banging a drum makes a deeply satisfying sound, which also effectively puts the teacher's voice beyond hearing, it is not surprising that often a child cannot or will not stop on request. Probably the best approach is the most obvious one, of restricting your players to one at a time; but try also to present the activity so that there is always the suggestion of something more interesting coming up next. For instance, with two or three children moving in turn round a varied collection of instruments, stopping, changing instruments, and starting again all on cue is less of a problem, because an instrument that someone else is playing is often more interesting than your own.

A foot-tapping exercise while pupils are sitting down is an excellent way of introducing rhythmic movement, but remember that this activity may be approached with enthusiasm partly because in most other classes it would be regarded as disruptive behaviour.

- Seat your children so that you can see their feet clearly, and ask them to try and tap alternate feet in time with a pulse – without at first lifting their heels from the floor.

- Modify the task: make it simpler or more difficult according to need, and do not be afraid to invent – or to encourage the children to invent – particular foot movements to suit exotic rhythms. Try them with a waltz, for instance, or a tango.

- Then move on to a marching and counting task: march on the spot for eight beats, for instance. Establish some ground rules; usually marchers begin with the left foot and, when marching on the spot, the arms may be moved in opposition to the legs, but it will probably be simpler at this stage if they are kept straight down by the sides.

- When you advance actually to marching round the room, the arms will need to be moved in opposition to provide balance. Try demonstrating eight paces across the room, with the right foot arriving at the side of the left on the last beat.

- Let the children take it in turns to play a large tom-tom or a bass drum, while others do the marching exercise.

To complete the link between marching in time, and playing the drum in time, it is important that everyone attempts to march while playing the pulse. This exercise may be expanded in subsequent lessons by introducing the side drum, and, if possible, a sling should be improvised so that the children can march a few paces, perhaps playing something other than the basic pulse provided by the bass drum. Simple drum technique should be introduced at this stage: loose wrists; alternate hands; the press roll; and the 'daddy–mammy' roll. Introduce and demonstrate these aspects of drumming for the children to try, but emphasise that the skills are of a high order, and not essential at this stage. The objective of this exercise is to establish a link between rhythmic movement and the sound of the drum.

Lesson 5
Rhythm and Pentatonic Melody

Position a bass xylophone in front of the class, and either a higher-pitched version or a glockenspiel nearby. Remove notes to leave the same pentatonic scale on both instruments.

Refer back to the heartbeat idea. Establish a pulse with a metronome, or clicking fingers; and demonstrate a simple, repeating bass pattern that you anticipate a pupil might be able to play. Ask for a volunteer, and if necessary simplify the pattern so that the pulse is maintained. Improvise a melody on the other instrument while the bass is playing. Begin with the same rhythmic pattern, then evolve a legato melody as if lifted into the air by the strength of the bass.

Monitor the pupils' reactions carefully. Even children of secondary school age who regard such instruments as childish will be fascinated at first by the gentle rhythm and tumbling harmonies of this pentatonic exercise. Try to persuade everyone to try the bass pattern, or, of course, to improvise their own, so long as it fits the pulse. Then let them try in turn to make a melody, over a rhythmic bass played either by you or by a reliable member of the group.

Make sure that everyone shares in the pleasure of the activity. Even children who cannot or will not take part must be included in a successful and enjoyable session by your gestures and comments, and the feelings displayed on your face.

Your language is particularly important. For many children music becomes more interesting when its elements are described in imaginative ways rather than the traditional formal terms, and Italian words. A tune may be lifted up on the bass pattern; it may be a big or small tune; it may call like a bird, or rattle like a collection of old bones; the bass may groan under its weight, or bounce along like father with his baby on his shoulders.

Children with restricted learning styles, particularly those whose interpretation of events is often too literal, may have difficulty in appreciating these links between sound and imagery, but it is worth persevering, using simple adjectives like 'big' and 'small' in situations where there is a clear link between the music and its shape and size.

Lesson 6
Rhythm Patterns
with Percussion Instruments

Arrange a selection of unpitched percussion instruments in front of the class. Begin the lesson by getting everyone to clap their hands in time, beginning after your introductory count. Then each pupil claps four beats only, in turn, without a pause so that the sound moves round the room. If they enjoy this you may like to try a round using the motif of four clapped beats, one group beginning their sequence one, two, or three beats after the other. Be prepared to accept that you may not be able to tell who is doing it correctly, and that you are likely to have pupils who deliberately clap in the wrong place to confuse you.

You may prefer to ask your children to practise instead by beating with alternate hands on their table tops. Beat out a simple rhythmic pattern on your desk using both hands, and ask individuals to imitate both the sound and the actions. Before you allow pupils to play the percussion, demonstrate how each instrument should be played and, in particular, how drum sticks should be held for best effect – ask them to try to play with loose wrists.

When the children are playing percussion, you must make allowances for their fascination with sonorous, percussive sounds. One or two players at a time is advisable, otherwise it may be difficult to get them to stop playing. At times, when a pulse or a rhythm seems to have taken over the lesson, you may find it both expedient and valuable to join in and let the experience develop until you feel, perhaps, that others are being unfairly excluded, or, better still, until the performance reaches its own natural point of decay.

- Play a simple one-bar pattern, and ask each player in turn to repeat it.

- If they are successful, repeat the pattern in time, and direct them to follow suit, so that a pulse is immediately implied.

- Call the name of the second player, and ask them to take over so that the pulse is maintained.

- Depending on the results of their efforts, introduce an easier, or more difficult, pattern, and begin the sequence again.

Change the players, giving each the same patterns to copy, and when everyone has tried, introduce the other percussion instruments, give everyone something to play, and try a group performance of the various motifs played as a question and answer sequence. Join the group, and let someone else try the solo part: encourage the players to try to maintain the pulse, even if they are having trouble with a particular pattern.

Lesson 7
Melody at the Keyboard (2)

Begin by drawing a much enlarged right hand on the blackboard, and assigning the first five notes of a major scale to the thumb and fingers. Write G next to the thumb; A next to the index finger, and so on. Put your hand on the board and demonstrate how each finger may move independently to play its note, singing as you play.

Ask the children to put their right hands flat on to their table tops, and devise a simple exercise involving lifting various fingers in turn. Call them by the note names, and, if left-handed children protest that it is too difficult, point out that they will have a considerable advantage when it comes to playing notes at the bottom end of the keyboard. Or, if you are working with children who will not be confused by the reversal, do the exercise with both hands, assigning G to the little finger of the left hand, and so on. It will probably be easier if you exercise all right hands together, and then the left.

There is scope here for finger play. The note names could be written on finger-nails, or labels may be stuck on fingers, or even simple paper puppets named according to their letter.

Sitting at the children's level, teach the song *Go Tell Aunt Nancy*, by singing and moving your fingers.

- Sing the note names at first rather than the words.

- Some children may be able to follow your finger movements, and sing the correct letters, but for most this is too complex a task; looking at their fingers and moving them in time, proscribes any further deliberate activity.

- At this point give the players copies of the note names so that they can process the information visually, while their ears are still assimilating the tune.

- Try to stay one step ahead of frustration or boredom, at all times.

The aim in this lesson is a performance of a tune by whatever means using fingers, toes or any other acceptable part of the anatomy. It is not essential to use consecutive fingers, but it is a useful technique, especially when children become more ambitious about the tunes that they want to play.

Play the tune on keyboards all together. Conduct, and sing the notes, making allowances for inaccurate note lengths, and erratic rhythm. Insist that the children stop when you cut them off – but don't expect miracles. Use a baton or a piece of dowelling that makes a distinctive noise when tapped on a table.

Teach them that this means: no noise, and ready to start.

It should be possible to direct an acceptable performance by dividing the tune between the players. It may be easiest to give each child one note to be played when directed, but some children will all too easily forget which is their note, and be unable to cope with the tension leading up to their brief moment of glory. Phrases are the most logical and satisfying way of dividing up the tune. After a little practice pupils can usually remember the shape and sound of their portion, and how it fits with the others to make a complete and balanced piece.

Some children may be happier if allowed to work in pairs at a keyboard, playing a phrase together in octaves, or, if the tune allows, in alternate notes. If this happens, try and ensure that they change places at some point so that both players experience the whole tune.

Arrange the seating in the room so that instruments may be passed from hand to hand without children having to leave their seats.

Place an assortment of unpitched percussion instruments on the table in front of a pupil who is sitting on the end of a row; it doesn't matter whether at the front or the back. Explain the activity. The children are to play the instrument that is passed to them until you shout or indicate 'change', then they receive another, and pass on their original instrument to the next person. During this excitement, they are to listen to the strongly rhythmic playing emerging from the teacher's piano, or keyboard, and try to keep in time with the pulse.

The instruments should be chosen for their distinctive and contrasting sounds, and before the fun begins it may be necessary to show pupils the most effective way of playing them, and to emphasise that instruments and beaters must be passed sensibly and not thrown.

Some children, especially when excited, cannot match their movements to a given pulse, and it may be helpful if they can see the teacher's arms and hands moving rhythmically at the keys. To this end, an electronic keyboard in full view of the class is clearly a more effective teaching aid than the traditional school piano.

The first child must decide from the selection on the table which instrument he or she will play first, and the teacher monitors the instruments' progress round the room until they accumulate on the table in front of the child at the end of the chain.

- Play a strong two-beat rhythm: the melody is not important. A simple bass figure with offbeat chords in the right hand is sufficient for this exercise, perhaps changing key at the moment of 'change'.

- After a time you may find that the pupils are not really listening to the music but are more involved with their social interaction.

- Extend the activity by asking them to change instruments when you change key, but make sure that you indicate the impending modulation with an easily recognisable motif each time.

You may like to vary the task by asking them to change when you stop playing. It is remarkable how children can focus their hearing in such situations, even when five or six instruments are playing together, and the teacher is playing very quietly.

Suggested instruments for this lesson are triangle; woodblock; scraper; maracas; a small drum; cowbell; finger cymbals.

Lesson 9
Conducting an Ensemble

If the class is not already familiar with the conventions
of conducting, spend some time in demonstrating the
gestures for beginning and ending a piece, and the
various expressive movements for variations in volume, pitch, and tempo. Exaggerate the movements,
partly because they are then easier to interpret, and
partly because children enjoy creating and changing
sound with a dramatic movement of the magic wand.

1. Distribute percussion instruments among
   the group, including drums, cymbals, and a
   miniature glockenspiel. Say how you would
   like each instrument to be played: the
   cymbal with a pair of soft beaters, for
   instance, or the triangle muffled by the
   hand.

2. Create a piece of mood music, selecting and
   pointing at the instruments that you want
   to hear, and starting and stopping each one
   before you move to another sound.

3. Allow each player an opportunity to try a
   gradual crescendo and diminuendo, and
   staccato notes which you pluck out of the
   air.

Show your pleasure at their performance, and move on to exploring combinations of sounds.

You may find that you have not enough hands to produce the desired effect, but encourage the children in their interpretation of your gestures, and try to use eye contact combined with movement to keep some instruments playing, while others make occasional interjections.

Change the players, and repeat the exercise. When all pupils have played, ask for volunteers to try conducting the group. Some children will have difficulty patterning your confident and expressive gestures. Help them briefly, perhaps by placing an arm at a more productive level, then retire and join the band.

- This activity may be extended by improvising music suggested by a theme. Everyone should be persuaded to take a turn with the baton, and to make a selection from a list of titles which might include *The Haunted House*, *The Night Train*, *The Invaders From Space* and *The Circus Comes to Town*.

You will need eight percussion instruments of contrasting sounds. Arrange them carelessly in a heap while you talk to the class about the lesson.

You are going to practise playing by numbers. It will be a little like painting with numbers in that each number will be represented by one sound. You explain to the children that most music is heard in pockets of time which are measured by counting, and you begin by demonstrating a simple one-in-the-bar beat on an instrument which can produce a well-defined pulse, and which does not need to be damped – perhaps a small drum.

1. Count and play: one; one; one; and so on, and explain that whoever plays the drum must be able to count and play when the counting goes back to that number. With some children you can illuminate the concept by singing an appropriate tune over each beat before they play, but others may be confused by the introduction of a new dimension into the activity. They will after all be simultaneously counting; searching for the pulse; and processing

feedback: a demanding combination for many pupils with special needs.

2. Hand the drum to a child, and make sure that you have enough room so that the players – eventually there will be eight – are able to stand in front of the class. Pick up a contrasting instrument, count a two-beat pulse, and play in opposition to the drum at least until you have established and maintained a good pulse.

3. The definition of percussion may be widened in this exercise to include a swanee whistle or siren. A contrasting sound of this kind seems to be particularly effective on the second beat; but when the activity is well under way, you may like to ask the players to judge on which beats the various instruments should play.

4. The exercise continues until you have eight children, each with a different instrument, playing and counting together to provide a continuous pulse. Take your time at each stage, making sure that the new count is well understood and established, before you add an instrument, and, in particular, remember to emphasise the appropriate beats in each set by your conducting, vocalising, and body language. Remember that while most adults and musicians would find five and seven beat bars

unusual if not uncomfortable, children who have a poorly developed sense of rhythm will probably find each of the patterns to be of equal difficulty. The act of repetitive counting, and the complexity of sounds that are being produced, may distract them from the task of following the pulse, but it would be counter-productive to expect more problems with five and seven, than with six or eight. Be careful what you say!

This is a demanding activity, but one which provides valuable exercise of a number of related skills, as well as amusement. It may be modified, if children cannot count and play, by the teacher counting aloud in front of the line of players and conducting each entry. But children who are confident and efficient may enjoy the challenge of being placed out of sequence, or of playing with their backs to each other so that they get no visual clues, and really have to count. With fewer than eight children you will have to restrict the number of beats, or ask some players to play more than one instrument. And although beginning with one beat and progressing to eight seems most convenient, you may of course choose to begin and end the exercise in different ways. Extending to ten beats may seem appealing, but in my experience it is virtually impossible to make ten distinctive percussion sounds with the battery available in most schools, and even less likely that your pupils will be able to play them in time, and perceive them as a pattern. The idea of the sequence of sounds as a pattern should be pursued as far as the children's developmental stages allow. Explain that one performance of a set or sequence could be described as a bar of music. An advanced group might attempt a performance of exactly eight bars, primed with your demonstration of the strategies musicians use to count bars.

Lesson 11
A Scale and Melody Patterns

Begin by teaching the C Major scale, demonstrating the conventional piano fingering, then ask the children to try. Move among the group putting fingers in place, and noting which children have most difficulty. Often such children are the ones who are most keen to try to do it properly, but emphasise that it is not essential, while pointing out the advantages of not having to look at your fingers each time a note is played.

It is important that you establish a link between sounds and position on the keyboard, and also that your pupils understand what is meant by high; low; up; down; melody; bass; and the term 'voice' on an electronic instrument. Allow them to practise the scale up and down with whichever hand is most convenient, then introduce a group test:

- Explain that you are going to make up a short tune using only the notes C, D, and E; and that you want them to put those three notes in the correct order to copy the tune.

- Sing your improvisation: E, D, C, for example, and give them a few seconds to practise and get the notes in the correct order.

This is one of the most frustrating exercises for all concerned, and although worth a try, it is probably not a practical proposition if there are more than two children in the group. There seem to be two major obstacles, either of which can provoke a negative attitude towards the activity. Many children, although they can sing with reasonable accuracy, are not aware that the notes of a tune move up and down, and would find difficulty in making a diagram of the shape of a melody. Second, some children who can demonstrate their understanding of the movement of a melody when sung may have a problem in translating its shape to that same unhelpful row of keys. That the notes may be found in a temporal pattern on the keys spread out before them is an idea that may require more than a casual introduction from a teacher for whom it is obvious.

Now teach or reinforce a simple tune; a nursery rhyme or a children's song that they have heard before. Choose a melody that at least begins with consecutive notes, so that the pupils are less likely to make mistakes when they begin the exercise. Make sure that they can all sing the tune, then give them the starting note, suggest which finger they should begin with, and ask them to try and pick out the tune – preferably wearing headphones.

This will prove to be a threatening exercise for some children, who may already have struggled with the preparatory work. It is a time for tact, and careful support:

- Stress that it is not a competition, and that they will quickly become proficient with practice.

- The ability to pick out a tune is highly valued by most children, and can provide a substantial boost to the confidence of a child who is doubtful about his or her ability.

Suggest that they sing and play until they become used to the sound of notes in unison, and try to hear each child while others in the group are busy, so that they may not feel unduly exposed. (A proper keyboard studio with facility for the teacher to listen to, and communicate with, individuals is, of course, the best situation for teaching at this level.) Remind them of the timing of the tune, and reinforce their efforts by singing the note names, and helping fingers into place where necessary.

A performance to the group may not be possible the first time, but if you have pupils who are good at this activity and wish to play their tunes to everyone, then try to encourage them without too much fuss. An egocentric child, whether able or not, may grow horns and a tail under the spotlight, or divert the interest and enthusiasm of classmates away from the task in hand.

Lesson 12
Listening to Recorded Music

It is difficult for most adults simply to sit and listen positively to recorded music, and one should not expect too much of children who will probably find it impossible to sit and do nothing, while trying to concentrate on unfamiliar sounds, without words or pictures. Whatever music you play should be short, aurally interesting, and, most important, should be related in your introduction to a colourful, and imaginative story – even if you have to make one up. Children seem to be able to hold quite complex orchestral sound patterns in their memories if there is an associated narrative or an emotional link. Most teenagers, for instance, can recognise the film music from the film *Jaws* after hearing only the first two ominous notes in the bass.

Having made the association with a story, there is a much better chance that your pupils will be able to remember some of the aural detail, whether it is the overall sound; the distinctive timbre of a particular instrument; the rhythmic movement of the piece; or a fragment of melody. After they have heard the music, your common experience will allow you to talk about it and you must give your pupils the opportunity to hear some of the language we use in referring to music.

It is essential, however, that, as well as introducing pupils to the common Italian terms, they are encouraged to express their ideas in their own words. Expressive and imaginative language is a much overlooked part of musical education, and you need only offer corrections when their use of language is plainly wrong. Often, for instance, children use 'slow' to mean 'quiet and soft'; and get muddled in their use of 'high' and 'low' because of the timbre of contrasting instruments.

You may like to ask your pupils to make expressive drawings while listening to the music. Often children can assimilate sounds while apparently engrossed in paper and pencil work, and some need to occupy their hands as if to block out distracting sensations and enable them to concentrate on the music. Others, however, will become so absorbed in the work of eyes and hands that they may become unaware of the music, as if they are doing homework at home with the television on in the corner of the room. This is a perennial problem, and probably best approached by making the point that listening to music in lessons is a special activity requiring a special skill. Active listening is difficult but rewarding, and you must promote it with each child depending on their individual needs. You may be surprised, however, how much of the music is received and remembered even when your pupils appear not to be listening. After you have played the piece two or three times in the first lesson, many

children are able to recognise it instantly after a few
bars when it is played again some weeks later.

1. Choose a piece – probably an excerpt –
   lasting about five minutes, and introduce it
   with a story. The first time it is played you
   should accompany the piece with a
   commentary, pointing out details such as
   particular instruments; a passage of sound
   painting; a recurring melodic motif; or
   landmarks in the musical narrative.

2. Ask your pupils to relax: perhaps even to sit
   with heads and arms on their tables, or just
   with eyes closed. Play the music, deliver
   your commentary, and note their responses.
   Talk briefly about their reactions when the
   music has finished, then ask them to draw;
   or to doodle in colour; or to write down
   words suggested by the sounds – and play
   the piece to them again.

3. Allow them to listen this time without your
   comments, then encourage the children to
   talk about their work, and to explain if
   possible which aspects of the music may be
   linked to the results. Be prepared for
   drawings or marks which are meaningless
   to you; which appear to be unrelated in any
   way to the music (except of course in time);
   which the child cannot explain; or those
   which reveal a train of thought completely
   alien to the musical experience. Teaching

music is more than music. You are a
development facilitator whose task is to
encourage communication and expression,
and you must give your pupils the
opportunity to hear music they would not
otherwise meet, even if you are met with
resistance and studied indifference. The
child who pretends not to be listening, and
who makes inappropriate marks on paper,
is expressing something, and is a part of the
experience that you have initiated.

As well as encouraging an expressive reaction from
your pupils, you should make points of information
about the music you choose for your listening sessions. They should be learning, for instance, to distin-
guish between the various instrumental groups, and
between individual instruments; how particular effects are produced; and to appreciate some of the
broad differences in musical styles throughout different cultures and times. Remember, however, that the
wide screen of chronological perception that we use is
irrelevant for most children with special needs. For
them Mozart may be simply as unfashionable as Brit-
ten: dead or alive makes no difference – although a
dramatic version of the former's life story like that
depicted in *Amadeus* may tease their interest long
enough for them to become interested in a piece of his
music.

The aim of music appreciation at this level must be
to elicit a response. If a child goes away humming a
tune; or vocalising a rhythm pattern; or responds in an

emotional way to a piece of music; or wants to write down the story, or draw a picture; or simply to talk about what he or she has heard; then progress is being made.

Lesson 13
Composing Simple Melodies

There are an infinite number of ways in which composition may be presented in the classroom. One may present pupils with a set of restrictions aimed at keeping the work simple, and focusing concentration; or, at the extreme, allow total freedom apart from setting a time limit for the completion of compositions. Because of the importance of responding effectively to individual needs, the teacher must be particularly sensitive to children's efforts at composition. The medium offers so many possibilities in the manipulation of its variables that often children are defeated by too much freedom in the early stages. It is wise to begin with lots of improvised examples; explain the restrictions, and why they are there; and then hover over shoulders with suggestions where necessary, encouragement, and more demonstrations.

1. Begin with an exercise using three consecutive notes, and ask the children to put them in a pleasing order, and to fit them into a rhythmic pattern so that it sounds right when repeated. Be careful not to show off in your demonstration. Some children will recognise instantly what is required;

others will find no merit in a piece of melody which sounds unlike anything they may have heard before. Beware the child of such a narrow musical and emotional experience that he or she cannot yet assimilate a new and strange tune, or even the idea that tunes may be composed. It may be necessary to teach pupils a rhythm pattern before presenting them with a melodic task, so that they have a firm base from which to start.

2. Alternatively you may choose to begin with an exercise similar to one used for shape finding in art, when children are asked to cover a page with a free and fluid scribble, and then the teacher helps them to find shapes and forms hiding in the marks. It requires the teacher's attention to be directed at one pupil for a time but can be rewarding with some children. Ask the child to play a handful of notes at random in a series of short exclamations, and stop him or her when you hear a combination that may stand alone as a musical motif. Then grab it quickly, before it escapes; write it down if necessary, sing it and teach it to the pupils until they can play it easily, and claim it as their own. Draw a parallel between such instant composition and other forms of improvised music. Point out

in

piec

comm.

3. Show tha
    being unrea
    idea how easy
    nor how far awa
    acclaim, really are.

Talk to your pupils about the   usic, and about musical associations. Ask   ether particular tunes bring back memories, or induce feelings, and try to make the point that such connections may be purely arbitrary, or coincidental; or the distinctive characteristics of the piece itself may have made a long lasting impression. It is a distinction which may be too subtle for many children, but one worth trying to make for those who will understand. A particular nursery rhyme, for instance, may stick in the memory because it was heard at mother's knee; but a different song heard under the same conditions may have been forgotten. The point is that there are qualities of music which appeal, and which may induce emotional reactions. Demonstrate what is meant by descriptive music, and explain that the composer is attempting to suggest a scene or a mood by the organisation of sounds, and play examples of those less easily defined

which suggest a scene
ience.

begin again to organise notes,
timulus of a scene, or a mood, and
again of the common musical associa-
and of the simple dimensions of their work:
igh – low; fast – slow; loud – soft. You might ask your
pupils for instance to compose a short lullaby – if it is
boring it may be more effective! Or a march; or a circus
piece; or an advertising jingle for margarine, or whatever product they may choose. The main objective of
the exercise is that their efforts should reach beyond
the classroom, if only in imagination, rather than ap-
pearing as the result of an intellectual exercise in jug-
gling notes.

Another way of beginning composition is to give your
pupils the first phrase of a simple tune such as *Twinkle
Twinkle*, and ask them to change one note. They must
record their altered version either on paper, or on their
electronic keyboard, so that they can reproduce it easily, and play it to the class. Then listen to all their
attempts, and ask if any of them sound like any other
tune, and which, if any, are still recognisable as *Twinkle
Twinkle*.

This exercise may be extended by asking your pupils to change more than one note in a particular
phrase, or one note in each phrase of a simple tune,
until you have results which are melodically far re-
moved from the original. It would obviously be un-
wise to choose for your raw material something with

a uniquely distinctive rhythm such as *Pop Goes the Weasel*, unless you wish to experiment with changing rhythmic emphasis; in this case, for example, offering the notes of the melody in duple time.

Lesson 14
Singing

Singing is such a fragile activity that no standard lesson can be relied on to be effective in all situations. For everyone except some categories of the disabled, the voice is the major channel through which we communicate emotion, sometimes in spite of our efforts. It is so easy for over-anxious singers to squeak, to mispitch a note, or to forget the words, that the teacher must display absolute faith in his or her pupils' ability to produce something of value. And, you must sing to your children, preferably with your ordinary speaking voice, and show how easy, and how natural, it is to sing.

You will meet with resistance, especially from boys with growly voices, but often from those whose voices have not yet broken, but who wish that they had growly voices too. Then there will always be children – usually girls – who want to sing and perform like their favourite pop stars; but between the refusers and the aspiring stars you may find a small voice of enough purity and accuracy to act as a vocal pilot in the group.

To begin where children are is a common and sensible response to teaching problems. Finding out where they are is a major problem in itself. You will want to begin singing as a group activity, but while children in mainstream classes can usually be persuaded to agree on a song or a style that takes their fancy, children with special needs often cannot. Perhaps because they are not sure what they like; or because they do not want to commit themselves before the others; or because for a variety of reasons they are anxious about the activity.

1. The first task then is to persuade them; to find a good excuse for a song, perhaps by making an association with a picture, or a story, or a situation that appeals to them. You might for instance, teach them *Land of The Silver Birch* if there is a canoeing trip in the offing; or a cowboy song if they are likely to have any experience of horseriding.

2. If your class can cope with the reading, display the words of the first verse using an overhead projector – or an A1 sheet. You may give the children copies if you wish, but sheets of paper easily become toys, and it is surprising how the quality of voices is diminished if heads are tilted downwards.

3. Read the words to them with the correct emphasis and rhythm; then ask them to join you and read them together. Check that every child is hearing you clearly, and saying the correct words. For some children poetic or lyric English is as foreign as French, and it is possible that they may mishear a word and replace it with

something familiar that has a similar sound, irrespective of meaning.

4. A song with words that can be chanted before being sung is particularly valuable, and you may extend the preliminary work by asking your group to whisper the words, with strong accents on the consonants. Remember, however, that you must be careful not to restrict the eventual performance by too many aesthetic considerations.

5. Sing the first verse to the class, preferably either unaccompanied or with a simple guitar accompaniment, and then ask them to join you and sing it again. If the song has a chorus, make a feature of it: say that everyone must sing the chorus; but don't make a fuss if they won't.

Use the piano sparingly: its volume, resonance, and in particular its percussive attack, are more likely to daunt anxious and insecure singers than provide support. Many songs require the merest glimmer of accompaniment to enliven an effective performance. A single note on a chime bar at each change of harmony may provide sufficient distraction from the singing to allow the voices to open, and the sounds to emerge. But do not allow your singing session to become a squabble over who plays what, and when. Your objective in the early sessions with a group should be to make active music making an enjoyable experience.

Do not rehearse too much; applaud every small achievement, and move on to the next line or verse; or to a discussion about which percussion instrument might enliven the performance; or to practise some movements to accompany the song; or to a real performance in front of a passing colleague, who may have been primed for just such an event.

Lesson 15
Musical Games and Group Activity

Music lessons provide an excellent opportunity for children to practise the skills of co-operation and communication, and for teachers the crucial skill of class management. Whether you work with your entire class throughout, or whether you organise different combinations of smaller groups, depends on numbers, ability, and the social mix; but whatever the situation, you should aim to encourage your pupils to listen to, and to consider the feelings and views of, others, while not suppressing their own. At the simplest level, a musical activity may consist of pupils sitting or standing together in a circle, and taking it in turns to make a noise with some part of their bodies. Apart from breaking wind, which is clearly not an act designed to promote group unity, anything goes.

- You may need to stress that body noise means using the resources of the player's own body, not percussive effects achieved by hitting others.

- With very immature children you may never get beyond imitations of excretory functions, but at least you will make the

point that everyone has to listen to the
others, and take their turn.

There is much scope for variation on this circle technique. You will devise activities to suit your circumstances, but never be afraid to experiment with new
ideas, or to borrow from other subjects or disciplines.
When working with children who have some rhythmic ability, for instance, but who need to practise
working with others, the following activity – bor-
rowed from a PE colleague – may be useful.

Working in a circle as before, the pupils bounce a
volleyball in turn, aiming to pass it to the next person
without losing the pulse. Some light and bouncy balls
make a satisfying noise when bounced, and if you
begin slowly with one bounce, and then a rest beat
while the ball is passed on, a steady swinging beat
may be established; and a group interest in maintain-
ing it.

Remember that the most successful activities con-
tain the seeds of their own decay, and that even a
bouncing exercise which succeeds beyond your hopes
will soon devolve to chaos. You may decide to allow
this natural event to take place, particularly if the
mood of the group is good, and everyone is enjoying
themselves; or, if rancour is emerging, to catch the
ball, and bring the activity neatly to an end before
presenting the next.

Group games with percussion instruments require as many different instruments as there are children, as well as a sensible blindfold. The following suggestions are intended to be used as stimuli for your own – or the children's – ideas.

1. All the children except one are dispersed around the room with their instruments, and the one remaining, after being blindfolded, is asked to find his or her way to the tambourine – with all the instruments playing together. There should be no obstacles in this game. The tambourine must be played continuously, but may of course be played very quietly next to an instrument the sound of which has a masking effect.

2. Again, one person is blindfolded, but this time is guided round tables and chairs by coded instructions on percussion instruments. A side drum beat means stop; a rattle on the tambourine means turn right; or, a ding on the triangle means go, for instance. This game works well as a team competition, working against the clock. It also makes an exciting simultaneous race; but you will need lots of space; a good selection of instruments; and children who can work together under the pressure of noise, and with adrenalin flowing.

3. One pupil waits outside the room while a suitable object is hidden inside. Then the others are each given an instrument, and when the searcher is brought back in, they indicate how near or how far away, by playing loudly or softly as he or she moves round the room.

4. Designate two or more groups, and give them all different instruments. Give each group a number between one and eight, and ask them to count up to eight over and over again, playing each time on their beats. Start them off with a metronome, or by playing the pulse yourself on a drum or on the piano. Or draw a simple graphic score on the blackboard or an OHP, with a part for each instrument, and a clear indication of the number of the beat on which they are required to play. Ideally this game should be easy enough for them to get it almost right straight away, but demanding enough for them to falter as soon as they appear to have mastered the technique of counting and playing together.

   Obvious variants of the game are performances with individuals playing on separate beats; or, for children with particularly tenacious minds, two numbers each.

What is likely to happen is that as the cross rhythms become more interesting, your pupils will learn their patterns and no longer need to count, so that they can appreciate what is going on around them, and perhaps even how their contribution fits into the overall sound. Then things may start to go wrong; and it is time for you to make the task easier, or more difficult; to change the patterns; to alter the speed of the pulse; or to lead the group into a new activity.

Lesson 16
A Group Performance

To move beyond impromptu games into a group musical performance requires a careful evaluation of objectives. You must decide whether all the pupils in the group are to play equal roles in the ensemble, in the knowledge that they are not equal in terms of ability, keenness, or social skills. It sounds like an impossible management task, but, in practice, each child is allowed an equal opportunity by rotating the instruments and the parts they are required to play.

In singing, for instance, you must offer the opportunity of a solo line or verse to each child in turn, without favouritism, and without making a fuss if a child refuses to sing. If you have a child who wants to sing solo all the time, you should be guided in your reaction by the attitudes expressed by the rest of the group. If they are supportive, you should offer the same opportunity to everyone, then set about organising some sort of accompaniment, so that your solo singers are still part of a group. Working with the mood of the class is an excellent general rule in music teaching, but remember that they may have just come from a lesson where their talents and abilities have been exposed in quite a different way, and they may carry prejudices with them into the classroom. You must draw them away from their squabbles and into

the proper spirit of music-making, beginning probably with the seating arrangements in the room.

If there are enough singers in your class to enable
you to divide the class into two groups, try them
singing alternate lines of a song while sitting on oppo-
site sides of the room. Not only can interesting musical effects be produced by moving voices around, but
you may note that the unity of the groups will be
affected by their position.

It is usually non-productive to emphasise direct
competition, and to announce winners and losers, but
there is a competitive element in all group performance, even at the professional orchestral level, with the
group competing with each other, and as a unit, to win
the attention and approbation of the audience.

With your class aroused and enthusiastic about
their music making, it would not be wise to try and
jerk them into reverse gear with an explanatory listening session, but you should point out in passing that
the idea of two or more groups, or an individual and
groups, all performing the same piece is one that is
expressed in music from many lands and cultures. The
element of competition is directed to a common aim:
the successful performance.

To conclude the group singing session you might
draw on an example from popular music for the class
to try: a soloist with crooning choir in the background,
for instance, or an outrageous send-up of a 'doowop'
song; but either of these suggestions needs research
and preparation, as well as a convincing soloist. A
more accessible alternative, particularly with the

boys, is likely to be a sea shanty with call and response. If you really have no one who can, or who will, call, then you must do it yourself. Stage the performance; record it if possible, and make sure that as much of your pupils' work as possible is saved on cassette, perhaps to be played to a wider audience.

Lesson 17
Shape, Pattern and Form

By referring to your pupils' experience across the curriculum, especially in Art, talk about, and define shape. Remember that even chaos has shape if it has boundaries on the map of our perceptions. Demonstrate some random, apparently chaotic, effects on your classroom instruments, and agree with your children on the type of events they have heard. Try and get them to use the appropriate words: loud, soft, short, long, high, low, for instance; and any expressive descriptions which they are able to offer. Try and provoke them by playing in ways that might be described as scary; frightening; gentle; bouncy; and so on.

Move on to talk about pattern, again drawing parallels with their artistic work, and other subjects. Agree on a working definition, but remember that children often do not appreciate the idea of pinning the meaning of a word down by defining it. Particularly for immature, or under-developed, minds, words change meaning depending on who is using them; on the circumstances; and on the direction of their widening experience.

Show your pupils some graphic patterns; and then try to demonstrate musical equivalents on a keyboard or percussion. From this point the lesson may move equally effectively in either of two main directions: either you give out paper and pencils or crayons, and ask the children to draw a pattern inspired by a piece of music; or you display a large, and preferably colourful, example of pattern in graphic art, and ask them to improvise a musical pattern suggested by what they can see.

Demonstrate a simple pattern inspired by a piece with clearly defined themes, such as the 'Entry of The Toreadors' from Bizet's *Carmen*. Play the music and draw a shape on the blackboard to represent the main tune. Draw the shape again when the tune repeats, and a different, perhaps smaller shape for the bridging theme before the main tune is heard again. Draw a contrasting shape for the legato tune in the next section – and so on, linking your shapes to produce a coherent overall design.

Another approach to this particular music would be to begin with an oval, or circular, shape to represent the bullring; and to set your design within the frame. Good artists may want to try to make accurate representations of the bull, the toreadors, and the matadors, but they should first complete the formal pattern-making process, using their own shapes while listening again to the music. You should find that no matter how involved children get with their drawing, they will still be able to appreciate the structure of the music.

Conclude the lesson by talking briefly about form, and this time making the point, if appropriate, that in music the term has a particular meaning which is more specific than its use in other contexts. If the concept is too sophisticated for your pupils, restrict yourself to a deeper exploration of pattern, especially in simple tunes. Show, for instance, how a tune such as *Pop Goes The Weasel* relies on repetition of melodic ideas which help us to remember the tune; and unexpected twists at the end of phrases, which help to retain our interest.

Lesson 18
Communicating Musical Ideas

You will need to build up a library of visual aids to demonstrate graphic communication by means of pattern; signs; symbols; and form. Your pupils may already know that music is traditionally represented on paper with notes, lines, dots and squiggles, and it may be useful to sketch the historical background of notation, showing examples of the earliest written music: especially those on illuminated manuscripts.

1. Show and demonstrate the connection between the position of note shapes on the paper, and the corresponding movement of a melody. Most children find this a sensible and easily grasped idea, but some have difficulty with the devices used to represent the passage of time, and the comparative length of notes. This is often an opportune moment to display and talk about some contemporary schemes of notation, in which the precise recording of the elements of a piece of music is replaced by a graphic display which is a stimulus for improvisation.

2. Give examples of graphic notation and play them; then ask your pupils for their suggestions, write them on the board, and get other children to interpret them. If they are still unsure of themselves, ask for specific shapes or patterns that might represent single musical events: a shape for a single short, loud noise, for instance. Or a symbol for a sound changing in pitch in a particular direction over three or four seconds. Then assemble an assortment of shapes on a scale marked clearly in seconds, start your metronome; or count; or better still, conduct; and direct a performance using voices, or body sounds, or whatever instruments the children suggest.

3. After two separate performances of the impromptu score from the blackboard or overhead projector, you may want to talk about the differences in the interpretations, and perhaps make changes in the notation system, and in the composition. Choose another conductor or director, re-assign the instruments, and make another performance.

Remember that the object of this lesson is to communicate to your pupils the value of musical notation. Make a permanent copy of your most successful piece, and if your children are able to make reasonably accurate marks on paper, get them to keep a record of their own. If you make a recording too, and keep it properly labelled in a place where you know you will be able to lay your hands on it instantly, you will be able to demonstrate the value of written music in a few weeks' time, when you are able to play the piece again from the notation, and compare it with the original performance. Ask your pupils for their comments. You may find that they point out some of the weaknesses of graphic notation, and suggest improvements: specific shapes, sizes, and colours, for instance, to represent particular effects or instruments; and a more efficient way of recording tempo and the comparative length of notes.

Remind your pupils of the virtues of conventional notation; while admitting its weaknesses. Demonstrate in particular the system by which the time value of notes is portrayed. Is there a better way of writing down a melody?

The concept of sound allied to graphics, or indeed any visual stimuli, is of particular value in teaching music to children with special needs. As well as asking children to draw and colour pictures while listening to music, I often borrow pieces of work done in their art lessons, and attempt with my classes to devise appropriate sounds to complement or enhance the pictures. This exercise is probably most effectively done using a video camera. Try a slow pan around a portrait, then zoom into a close-up accompanied by pastoral or sad music, or by angry or energetic sounds. There is scope here for work using more complex imagery, even to the point of making a short video film with music and pictures conceived, arranged, and executed by pupils.

Lesson 19
Making Patterns with Noises

Play a piece of *musique concrète*, or any piece consisting of organised contrasting noises, and talk about it with your group. Try not to get involved in a discussion about likes and dislikes, or good and bad music, but draw attention to the sounds and the way that they are arranged. Remind them that a tune is a pattern of pitched notes, and a rhythm is a pattern of beats. Were there any patterns in the music that they have been listening to?

1. To make sure that everyone understands, contrive some contrasting noises – not with instruments – and organise them into some sort of pattern involving the elements of time, volume, and pitch. Use whatever utensils and equipment are available in the room, but practise beforehand, preferably alone. (I once wanted to add the sound of a slamming door to a piece of music I was conducting but I slammed too hard and got, not only a satisfying bang, but also the sound of breaking glass as the entire top panel of the door fell on to the concrete floor outside!)

For more convenient and controllable noises try:

- rulers twanging or slapping

- furniture creaking

- ballpoints clicking

- a large sheet of card vibrating between the hands

- paper rattling

- water shaking in a bottle

- plastic bottle tops unscrewing

- electronic noises, such as white noise on a radio, alarms on wristwatches and sampled or synthesised sounds on a keyboard.

Give everyone a chance to make some noises, and to make suggestions for organising them.

2. Remind your pupils of the important elements of form in music: repetition and sequence; contrast and brevity; all bound by an organising principle, which in these exercises will probably be anything other than a key centre.

There will of course be lots of opportunity in this lesson for noisy mischief. You must endeavour to be firm, flexible, and fair. Accept all practical suggestions for noises – but keep all fragile equipment out of harm's way. There will often be those who want to tear up a book, or break a window, and you might invite them to tear up an old telephone directory, and ask for suggestions for noises which imitate the sound of breaking glass. There are recordings of sound effects available which might be useful, and for the breaking glass noise you might experiment with nails or pebbles dropping on to a metal sheet, or being shaken in a metal bin.

The scope for manipulating sound is now virtually limitless given the sophistication of modern technology, but teachers working as I do with a gramophone, cassette deck, and a radio-cassette need not feel deprived. The object of the noise lesson is to explore the possibilities of organising sounds into patterns which might be described as musical, and pupils are usually happy to use the most basic of equipment – provided that it works.

Lesson 20
Sounds and Communication

Sound is such a dominant part of our communication system that a series of lessons may be devoted to examining the meanings we commonly attach to noises. You will need to spend some time collecting samples, but the field is rich in variety and interest. Local noises may have particular significance for your pupils, for example:

- fire engine/ambulance/police car

- trains – electric, diesel or steam

- river traffic and water sounds

- supermarket tills

- traffic noises

- birdsong

- water boiling

- gas cooker lighting and burning

- boiling and frying noises

- crockery and utensils rattling

- paper, foil or plastic wrappers being torn open

- sauce glopping

- feet on gravel, footsteps on stone

- babies and children crying, laughing or talking.

Try to compile taped examples of noises and effects, and if possible enlist the aid of pupils in adding to your collection. You should of course have access to a good quality portable recording machine, and facilities for mixing and editing. With more sophisticated equipment at your disposal you may even be able to transform your raw material electronically but do not allow the technology to seduce you away from your objectives: to allow your pupils to explore the expressive and emotive capacity of everyday sounds.

Remember that reactions to sounds are unique, and take care when working with disturbed children that they are not made to feel anxious or vulnerable by being exposed to a noise which has unhappy or threatening associations for them. Those sounds which have obvious emotional content should be used with care, but it may be helpful and therapeutic to encourage the use of poignant or threatening sounds in a composition. With a sensitive child the teacher must take note of the reaction and take cues from the pupil. A sound which produces a doubtful reaction may be rendered harmless or even comic by repetition; or by mixing it with something else; or by fading it into a more comforting sound. The exercise belongs to your pupils. Encourage their decisions, applaud them, and, as always, give equal value to all individual efforts.

I have suggested collecting sounds, and the possibility – depending on the facilities available – of editing, mixing, and organising them into meaningful or musical sequences which might be narrative or expressive in content. You may prefer, however, to concentrate on the listening and interpretative aspect, and ask your pupils to talk about sounds that you have played; or to respond with art work or expressive writing; or to suggest some movement that might complement what they have heard. There are lots of possibilities, some of which may lead your teaching away from music; but try to be pragmatic, and to keep the welfare and development of your pupils foremost in your mind. The aim of all the activities is to promote and enhance growth, and in particular to encourage self-expression and self-understanding through reacting to sounds. If your efforts and the reactions of your pupils lead you away from the conventional idea of a music lesson, then think again about your perception of the medium. Why should the sound of a mountain stream be regarded as musical, and not the angry sound of a car racing, brakes squealing, and crashing? Why the music of laughter, and the noise of a child crying?

To imply a definition of music as a parcel of sound – whether organised or not – and to bring out into the open its efficiency as a medium of emotion may challenge and threaten your pupils. You should proceed with extreme caution, taking into account the sophistication and conceptual ability of your pupils. On hearing a recording of someone crying, for instance, you may find children who profess delight in the pain and misfortune of others; and their reactions may be genuine, and not just contrived to annoy the teacher. At such times you must remain dispassionate, and not express your feelings. Calmly reiterate your belief that to meet and know the strength and direction of one's emotions is a valuable experience; and if a debate is difficult to avoid, ask for a response from those children in the group who are compassionate and sensitive to the feelings of others.

CHAPTER 3

Record Keeping

Attitudes towards record keeping by teachers have changed dramatically over the last few years. Or perhaps it would be more accurate to say that central government, in its search for resonance with a public need, has demanded that teachers are more accountable, and that every child's progress shall be charted and measured throughout his or her school career. Teachers' attitudes, however, are not easily changed by political decisions, and there has been a great deal of resistance to change, and debate about the nature and value of tests and records of achievement. Setting aside the problem of the time required by teachers to test large numbers of children, a major axis of the debate has been the value of presenting children at particular milestones in their careers with formal tests issuing from a central curricular body, with a view of making comparisons, and drawing up league tables of school performance.

We need not enter into the debate here except to say that, in dealing with children with special needs, who are all in some degree disabled learners, it is odious to make comparisons in attainment. Music teachers need to be able to talk to the child's parents in their own terms about musical activities, and to show how the pupil's performance and attainment are related to their subject areas, and to his or her overall development. We must be able to explain why we do things, and perhaps to suggest ways in which parents can reinforce our efforts at home, while the attitude and self-image of the pupil remains our central concern.

You must keep a record of your lessons, and of the performance of your pupils, even if it is only in the form of a diary in which you make comments and recommendations. Whatever system you use you should, after a term, be able to give a detailed report on any pupil's strengths and weaknesses in your lessons.

- You should be able to say whether a child is right or left handed, and comment on the degree of dominance or weakness when playing percussion instruments.

- You should be able to comment on the dexterity of their fingers, and the degree to which they are able to use fine motor control – as in a five-finger exercise for instance.

- You should have recorded how well they move in marching or dancing exercises, and how responsive they appear to be to the pulse of accompanying music.

- You will have noted how well each child can play a drum in time, how well each is able to respond to a given rhythmic pattern, and you will be able to make some assessment of a pupil's short-term memory based on rhythmic and melodic exercises.

- You will know which of your pupils can remember the notes of a tune, which of them can pick them out again at a keyboard, and which children are able to reproduce a melody entirely by ear.

- You should be able to say which children are capable of performing at some level before an audience, and know which of your pupils have had difficulty in working with others, or perhaps in sharing an instrument.

- You will have some idea of your pupil's imaginative powers through their use of music as a descriptive or expressive medium, and you should know to what extent they are able to communicate their feelings about music in graphic form, and to relate and compare pattern and shape in music to forms in other subject areas.

It is possible to devise standard tests along the lines of those used to test reading, spelling or numeracy. The graded tests of the Associated Board, for instance, are indicators of levels of ability in clearly defined areas of musical knowledge and performance. They are not intended as diagnostic tests, but as records of progress and evidence of achievement on a strictly limited scale. Since musical activity throughout this book is regarded as a medium of communication, and an essential tool in the promotion of healthy growth in children, such tests are of little value in themselves. Pupils, however, love to receive certificates for achievement, and you may wish to adapt the examples in the appendix for your own use, or design your own. A moment's consideration will reveal the extent of the task. The document should be specific about what has been achieved, but a child struggling to play *Twinkle Twinkle* with one finger may be mature enough to place little value on a certificate which records the fact. Or if your version records that the pupil was able to play a simple tune accurately, how strict will you be on tempo, timing and rhythm? Perhaps the fairest system of certificates for achievement would be to design a series for every individual, but in that case how would they carry any effective validation from your school or local authority? In my experience most children love to compete, provided they can feel that they are doing so on equal terms, and that there is some protection against the feelings of failure and hopelessness which are all too familiar aspects of their experience. This is a difficult state to achieve with a group of individuals, all with unique special needs, and you may feel that, however carefully certificates of achievement are written, the element of competition is difficult to avoid, and inappropriate or even harmful. A document which is set at a level which will allow every child in the group to receive the award will be valued by some of your pupils, but others will be more cynical, and regard the exercise as if it were a children's party game in which everyone gets a prize.

The simplest and most effective form of record keeping is a note made by the teacher, during a session or immediately afterwards, of the stimulus presented by the teacher; the child's response; and the character of the relationship at that time. This is only possible, of course, if you are fortunate enough to be teaching individuals, or very small groups, in which case you should be in a position to construct individual programmes of activity for each pupil, and to keep fairly detailed notes as your series of lessons proceeds. No separate testing should be necessary since your records should show all essential information. If, for instance, you were trying to get a pupil used to using short-term memory for a musical task, you would record the task; the pupil's response in terms of character, and quality; and a comment about the quality of your relationship with the pupil during the session. This last item may seem idiosyncratic, but bear in mind that in such an intensive teaching experience the

pupil's response depends as much on your management of your relationship as on formal preparation
and presentation.

You must, however, be sure that your notes for each
child have some reference to your aims and objectives.

- If you are fortunate enough to be teaching
  individuals, or very small groups, you will
  have constructed a different programme of
  work for each child, after consultation with
  other professionals, and the appropriate
  negotiation with the child. At this intensive
  level of working, record keeping should
  provide a complete word picture of your
  relationship with your pupil, and there will
  be no need for separate tests at intervals in
  order to measure progress.

- With larger groups, perhaps of more than
  four, it will be necessary to construct simple
  tests which complement your teaching, and
  which allow you to record progress with a
  symbol of some kind, since there will not be
  time for you to teach, observe, and write
  notes on each child either during the lesson
  or immediately afterwards.

It is sometimes difficult to keep your objectives in
mind. You should be able at any time to describe a
pupil's current stage of development with reference to
progress made in your lessons, and to suggest a range

of future activities with a view to aiding particular aspects of development. You need records which will show:

- who was present in your lesson

- the activities they took part in

- how well they performed

- the success or failure of the lesson from your point of view, based on the mood and temper of your pupils, and their overall performance.

You must decide first how much space you need for each pupil's record, and whether your notes on a small group can be kept effectively on one sheet of paper. A page for each child may seem a good idea, but you may not have time to fill the space, and finding the appropriate page when you are under pressure may prove to be a frustrating exercise that affects your judgement. Experiment with grids containing boxes of different sizes, and decide how much information you can fairly hope to get on one page – and keep in mind the time dimension. My own system is still evolving, but at the moment I use a single sheet of A4 each half term for my groups of 8–10 children, turning over the page after the break. At the end of the year I will have each child's record spread across six sides, and it is fairly easy to summarise, and make assessments from information which has been recorded in this form.

CONFIDENTIALITY

It is my view that parents should have easy access to whatever notes that teachers have made about their children. If you have a good and proper relationship with parents, most will be satisfied with your yearly summary, and a verbal report on parents' evenings, but you must be prepared at all times to show them your records, and to explain whatever system you have devised.

It may be argued that children too should have access to their own records, but where children with special needs are concerned I believe it safer to restrict access, except as a result of parents' express wishes. It is difficult to imagine a practical system of record keeping which did not include marks, or comments at levels of achievement, and it would be natural for a child reading such records to want to compare their performance with others. Children with special needs are often unable to make accurate assessments of their efforts and potential, and although the teacher should always make it plain to pupils what has been written about them, it is usually inappropriate to let children see raw marks, or comparative comments – even in code.

RECORDING STYLES – SYMBOLS, NUMBERS, OR WORDS

At the other extreme to the simple grid suggested above, lies the detailed list of skills which requires only a tick to be inserted in the appropriate box. My example was used with limited success for a year or two, before being discarded in favour of the current version which allows me to make brief comments about a child's performance on a particular task. The obvious disadvantage of the skills chart is that it takes two sides of A4 for each child, and there is little room for anything other than ticks, or marks. What I did not find out until I tried to use these sheets, however, is that no matter how hard I tried to break down and classify the skills involved, the children defeated my system by refusing to conform to my steps, or my sequence. Some children never got past Step 1 on my chart, or did so at some times but not at others; while other children invented new categories of skills, usually falling in between mine, which would have made a more comprehensive chart too long and complicated to be of practical use. Some mainstream schools use lists like this in other subjects, and with groups of 20 or more they may be useful; but children who are disabled learners need a more sensitive response to their efforts. It is not enough to say that a child succeeded or failed at a task on one particular day by means of a tick on a grid, but, unless you have time to write detailed notes during or immediately after each lesson, then you may find it difficult to record what each child did, and how well it was done.

Your compromise, using the most useful elements of the systems used by other teachers, should be made with reference to the following factors:

1. The size of your groups.

2. The total number of pupils in your music
    lessons.

3. The need to record activities – some of which
    are more important in diagnostic and
    developmental terms than others.

4. The need to map, balance, and evaluate your
    teaching.

5. The need to communicate effectively with
    parents about their child's attitude, and
    progress.

6. The need to communicate positively with
    your pupils about their efforts and
    progress; it is easy to make unfair
    judgements about children's work because
    of your preconceived ideas about their
    ability.

Your system should allow you to record information
simply and effectively, so that it may be easily recalled
at a later date. Some teachers use tick lists, or award
scores for attainment in certain exercises; others es-
chew the formality of such an approach, and prefer to
write brief comments about each pupil. In the major
subject areas, current practice for Records Of Achievement requires each child to be aware of the content
and the objectives of their lessons, and to award themselves a score, or at least make a comment about their
performance at the end of a term. Probably the most

useful practice is a combination of techniques, since what is being recorded is information about a wide range of abilities in various situations. Your pupils should know that they will be expected to perform a tune after a term's lessons, for instance, and they will be able to make their own assessment of their progress after that time.

Your private records, however, might show a simple mark out of ten for each child so that you know which of them may need help in future tasks involving melody; and a supporting comment about the way in which the score was achieved, or about the style and confidence of the performance. It is an onerous task, but important if the teacher is to make assessments, and plan strategies for pupils who need extra help. You are not simply a teacher of music, but a teacher of children with special needs, and you must try always to be aware of your pupils' problems, and progress in other subjects, but principally in reading, language, and expression. I use the term 'expression' rather than 'communication' in the belief that a child who is able to express his feelings is on the way to coming to terms with his or her problems, whereas communication is received from many children via an iron mask, or a rigid behaviour pattern. You should take every opportunity to talk to colleagues about your pupils' progress in other disciplines. Find out what topics they are pursuing, and always be watchful for links which may be made: with the idea of pattern, for instance; or growth; or colour; or families; or the measurement of time.

You may have less than an hour a week with each group of children. Set that against all their other activities, in and out of school, and you will see that for many children music lessons are an insignificant part of their lives. You will be working, furthermore, with children who have been brought up on convenience foods, and instant entertainment, some of whom expect an electronic keyboard to play a complete tune in several parts at the touch of a key. You will have an uphill journey: but at least the path is clear.

- You will introduce them to new emotional experiences, and show them how familiar feelings can be transformed through music.

- You will show them how we can communicate with instruments, and share feelings as part of an audience.

- You should not present yourself as some great panjandrum of the art, but as someone who enjoys playing and listening to music, and talking about it to children.

- You will aim to promote the development of your pupils beyond the confines of subject areas, and if on the way you succeed in creating a moment or two of magic in your classroom, then you will have made an indelible mark, and know your reward.

Appendices

1. An example of a comprehensive individual record sheet

2. An opportunity for pupils to respond to the music course

3. A more formal record sheet

An Example of a Comprehensive Individual Record Sheet

Individual Record

Name:. . . . . Date:. . . . .

Right/Left Handed:. . . . .
. . . . Dominance/Weakness: . . . . . .
. . . .
. . . .
. . . .

Co-ordination/Gross Motor Control: . . . .
. . . .
. . . .
. . . .

Beating a drum:. . . . .
. . . .
. . . .
. . . .

Beating in time: . . . .
. . . .
. . . .
. . . .

Echoing a given rhythm pattern: . . . .
. . . .
. . . .
. . . .

Responding to a given rhythm pattern: . . . .
. . . .
. . . .
. . . .

Initiating a rhythm pattern:. . . . .
. . . .
. . . .
. . . .

Clapping hands in time: . . . .
. . . .
. . . .
. . . .

Stamping feet in time: . . . .
. . . .
. . . .
. . . .

Marching:. . . . .
. . . .
. . . .
. . . .

Dancing:. . . . .
. . . .
. . . .
. . . .

Melody Recognition: . . . .
. . . .
. . . .
. . . .

Memory of note-name sequences: . . . .
. . . .
. . . .
. . . .

Playing by ear:. . . . .
. . . .
. . . .
. . . .

Singing:. . . . .
. . . .
. . . .
. . . .

Playing a tune in time/with a pulse:. . . . .
. . . .
. . . .
. . . .

Working with others: . . . .
. . . .
. . . .
. . . .

Performing before an audience: . . . .
. . . .
. . . .
. . . .

Response to music:

Oral: . . . .
. . . .
. . . .
. . . .

Graphic: . . . .
. . . .
. . . .
. . . .

Physical/Emotional: . . . .
. . . .
. . . .
. . . .

Discerning pattern and form: . . . .
. . . .
. . . .
. . . .

Composing/arranging/improvising/conducting: . .
. . . .
. . . .
. . . .
. . . .

Musical responses to visual/verbal stimuli: . . . . . .
. . . .
. . . .
. . . .
. . . .

Attitude to the lessons – and response: . . . .
. . . .
. . . .
. . . .
. . . .

Relationship with peers in the lesson; and with the
teacher: . . . .
. . . .
. . . .
. . . .
. . . .

An Opportunity for Pupils to Respond to the Music Course

The teacher may wish to comment on the child's marks, either by adding his or her marks alongside those of the pupil, or by a comment at the bottom of the sheet.

Music................................... Term

Name:................. Date:...............

I have played (instruments):...................

....

....

....

I have played (tunes):. . . . .
. . . .
. . . .
. . . .

I have sung: . . . .
. . . .
. . . .
. . . .

I have conducted/improvised:. . . . .
. . . .
. . . .
. . . .

I have listened to: . . . .
. . . .
. . . .
. . . .

I most enjoyed: . . . .
. . . .
. . . .
. . . .

I did not enjoy: ....
....
....
....

My marks out of five:

Playing percussion:

Playing melody instruments:

Listening and responding:

Creating music:

Trying hard:

Teacher's comments: ....
....
....
....
....
....
....
....
....
....
....

A Formal Record Sheet

This has the advantage of a simple presentation of the basic syllabus but, it is inflexible in use.

Music Syllabus/Record Sheets

Name: . . . .

Rhythm: formal (*or any percussion instrument with hands or beaters)

1. Strikes a drum* cleanly with either hand.

2. Strikes a drum loudly or softly on request.

3. Strikes a drum on time after an introductory count.

4. Strikes a drum as directed by a conductor.

5. Plays four or more crotchet beats in time.

6. Plays quaver, quaver, crotchet, crotchet, crotchet in time.

7. Plays crotchet, quaver, quaver, crotchet, crotchet in time.

8. Plays crotchet, crotchet, quaver, quaver, crotchet in time.

9. Plays crotchet, crotchet, crotchet, quaver, quaver in time.

10. Plays 6, 7, 8 or 9 in good time for at least 1 minute at $\quarternote$ = 120.

11. Plays as 10 but using alternate hands for part of the pattern.

12. Plays a quaver triplet and 3 crotchets: the triplet on beats 1, 2, 3 or 4.

13. Plays 12 in good time for at least 1 minute at $\quarternote$ = 120.

14. Plays 4 semi-quavers and 3 crotchets: the semi-quavers on beats 1, 2, 3 or 4.

15. Plays 14 in good time for at least 1 minute at any speed.

16. Plays separate matching pulses with two hands, or with hand and foot.

17. Plays a roll correctly with both hands.

18. Sustains a relaxed and controlled roll for at least 1 minute with dynamics as 23.

Rhythm: expression and improvisation

19. Improvises a coherent rhythm pattern and repeats it on request.

20. Improvises a coherent rhythm pattern to accompany another instrument.

21. Improvises a rhythm or effect to enhance a mood or a sound picture.

22. Starts and stops on the direction of a conductor.

23. Understands and plays crescendo and descrescendo under a conductor.

24. Starts, stops, and conducts an ensemble with simple dynamics.

25. Directs an ensemble with sensitivity to create a mood or sound-track.

Melody

1. Plays up to four notes in time from dictation.

2. Plays up to five notes from letter names.

3. Plays a simple tune from letter names, accurately and in time. (Twinkle; Kumbaya; etc.)

4. Plays a melody with others under the direction of a conductor.

5. Plays a simple tune accurately by ear.

6. Plays a simple tune with one finger automatic accompaniment, in good time, tempo, and rhythm.

7. Plays a simple tune with one hand playing chords.

8. Plays an AB tune from letter names, accurately and in time.

9. Plays an AB tune accurately with manual or automatic accompaniment.

10. Improvises with melody and timbre to illustrate a mood, theme or situation.

11. Composes a tune with shape, pattern and sequence; and plays it in time.

Singing

12. Sings with the full choir.

13. Sings a verse or part in a small group.

14. Sings a solo verse or part with the choir.

15. Sings a solo song before an audience of peers and teachers.

16. Sings a solo before a public audience.

Conducting

17. Starts and stops an ensemble.

18. Beats time accurately.

19. Beats time and indicates dynamics and tempo changes.

20. Beats time, selecting and prompting players within the ensemble.

21. Beats time and indicates the beats of the bars.

Composing

22. Composes *in situ* by conducting an ensemble.

23. Improvises on an instrument around a theme or stimulus.

24. Works on a piece throughout a session to refine shape, form, and texture.

25. Composes and notates a piece of music, then reproduces it accurately later.

26. Puts together words and music to make a song.

27. Notates the song and reproduces it accurately later.